2nd Edition

Ξ 1B

T0012401

Succeeding with a Notespeller

by Helen Marlais with Cynthia Coster

Production: Frank J. Hackinson
Production Coordinators: Peggy Gallagher and Philip Groeber
Editors: Peggy Gallagher and Edwin McLean
Cover Art Concept: Helen Marlais
Cover and Interior Illustrations: ©2011 Melissa L. Ballard, Las Flores, California
Cover and Interior Illustration Concepts: Helen Marlais and Cynthia Coster
Engraving: Tempo Music Press, Inc.
Printer: Tempo Music Press, Inc.

THE FJH MUSIC COMPANY INC.
Frank J. Hackinson

ISBN-13: 978-1-61928-270-4

Table of Contents

Correlates to 2nd Edition, SATP®, Lesson and Technique Book, Grade 1B

FJH2329

Treble C Position

How fast can you find the Treble C patterns?

- Draw a line from the square on the left that matches the pattern of notes in the circle on the right.
- Then name the notes.

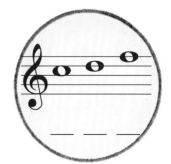

The Road to Good Reading

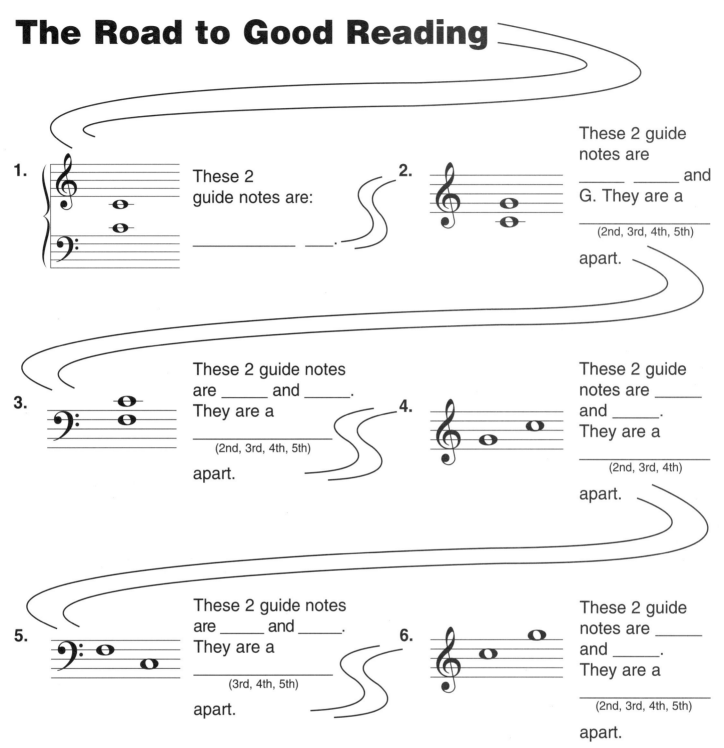

1. These 2 guide notes are:

_____ _____ .

2. These 2 guide notes are _____ _____ and G. They are a _____ (2nd, 3rd, 4th, 5th) apart.

3. These 2 guide notes are _____ and _____. They are a _____ (2nd, 3rd, 4th, 5th) apart.

4. These 2 guide notes are _____ and _____. They are a _____ (2nd, 3rd, 4th) apart.

5. These 2 guide notes are _____ and _____. They are a _____ (3rd, 4th, 5th) apart.

6. These 2 guide notes are _____ and _____. They are a _____ (2nd, 3rd, 4th, 5th) apart.

You can learn all the notes on the staff by using guide notes!

Ex.

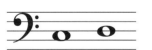

Guide Note C.
Up a 2nd is a __D__ .

The 1st note
is Guide Note _____.
Up a 3rd is _____.

The 1st note
is Guide Note _____.
Down a 4th is _____.

FJH2329

Wow! I Know My Intervals!

1. Draw 2nds from the smiley face notes.
Then name the notes.

up a 2nd	down a 2nd	down a 2nd	up a 2nd

___ ___   ___ ___   ___ ___   ___ ___

2. Draw 3rds from the star notes.
Then name the notes.

down a 3rd	up a 3rd	down a 3rd	up a 3rd

___ ___   ___ ___   ___ ___   ___ ___

3. Draw 4ths from the triangle notes.
Then name the notes.

up a 4th	down a 4th	up a 4th	down a 4th

___ ___   ___ ___   ___ ___   ___ ___

4. Draw 5ths from the square notes.
Then name the notes.

up a 5th	down a 5th	down a 5th	up a 5th

___ ___   ___ ___   ___ ___   ___ ___

G Position
Pogo Stick Jumps

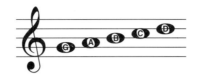

Name the notes on each keyboard and draw them on the staff.

Do you know why…   Lily likes line notes and   Sally likes space notes?

(Answer is below)

Answer: "Lily" begins with "L." "Sally" begins with "S."

Draw the G Position notes on the staff. Use whole notes.

G   B   D   A   C   G   D   A   B   G   C   A

FJH2329

More Pogo Stick Fun

Name the notes on each keyboard and draw them on the staff.

Draw the G Position notes on the staff. Use quarter notes.

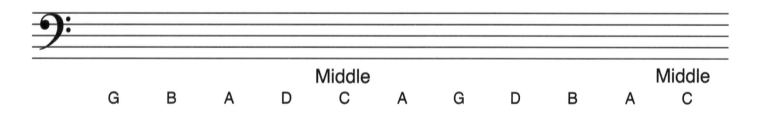

G Position Oasis

Name the intervals and notes in each water urn.

Ex.

4th

A D

FJH2329

Sharps Go Up!

- When you see a ♯, go up one half step to find the correct key – it's easy.

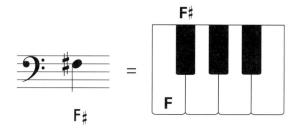

Name each sharp black key on the keyboard below.

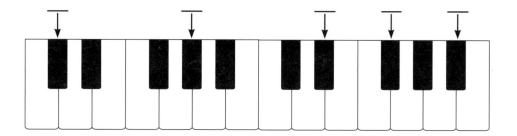

- Three of the following notes are not correct. Cross them out and label them correctly. Then play the correct notes.

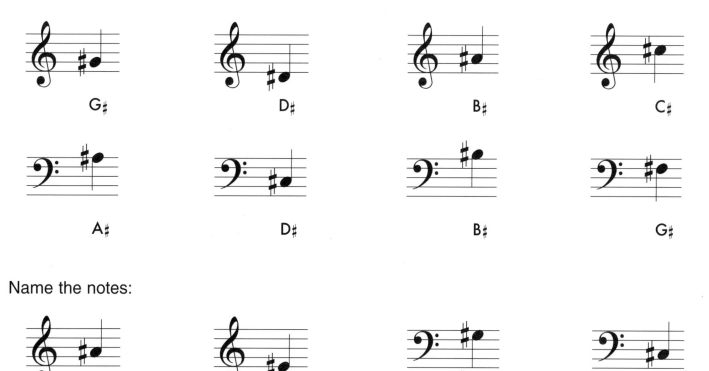

Name the notes:

Which of these sharped notes is a **white** key? _____

Half Steps

Bunnies and Half Steps

Bunnies like half steps (from 1 key to the very next key.)
Use this keyboard to help you with the following activities.

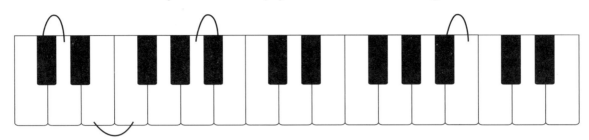

Draw a note a half step **higher** and then name both notes. Use half notes.

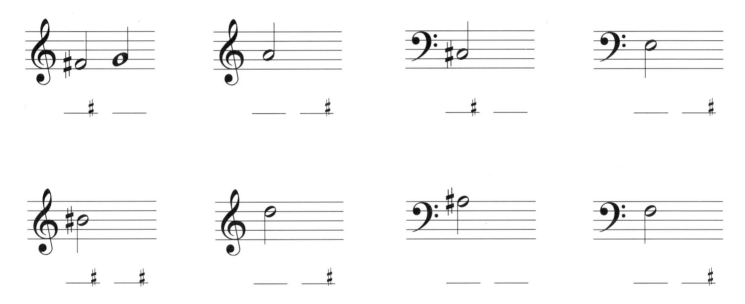

Draw a note a half step **lower** and then name both notes. Use quarter notes.

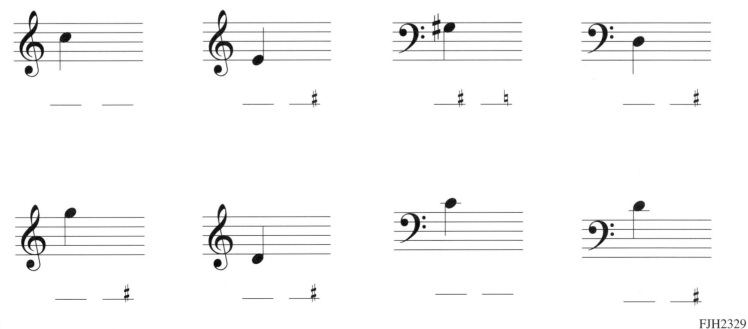

FJH2329

Juggling Sharps

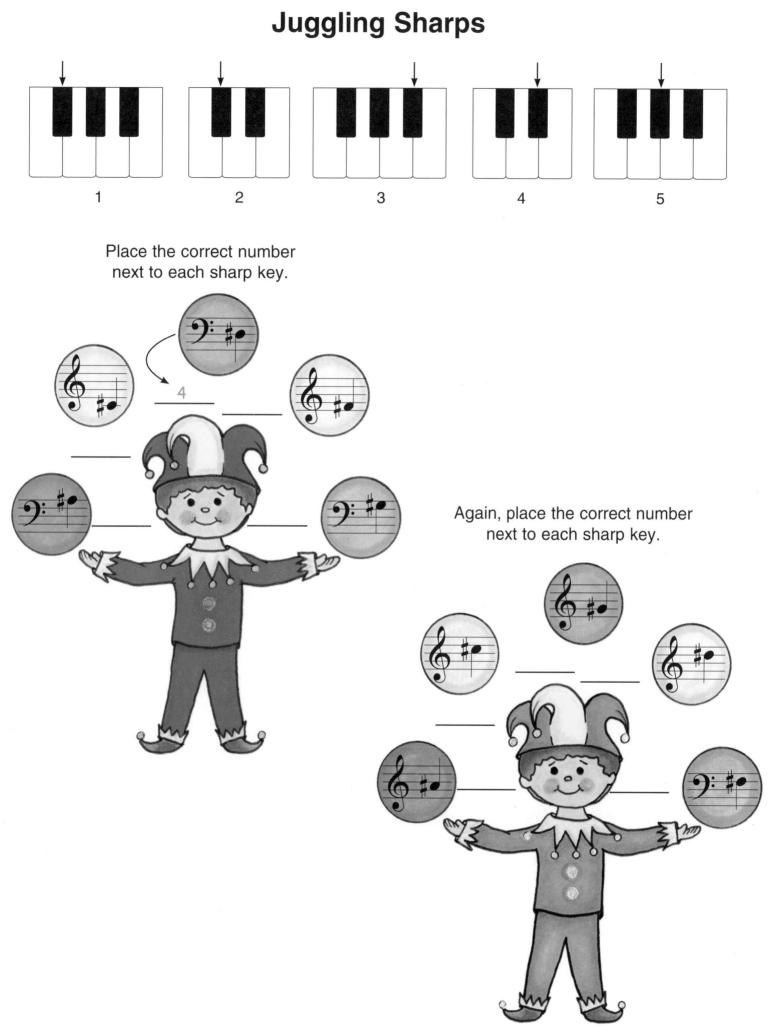

Place the correct number
next to each sharp key.

Again, place the correct number
next to each sharp key.

Flats Go Down!

- When you see a ♭, go down one half step to find the correct key – it's easy.

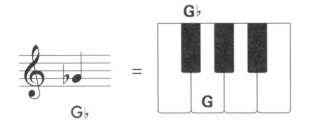

Name each flat black key on the keyboard below.

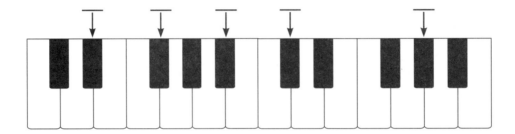

- Three of the following notes are not correct. Cross them out and label them correctly. Then play the correct notes.

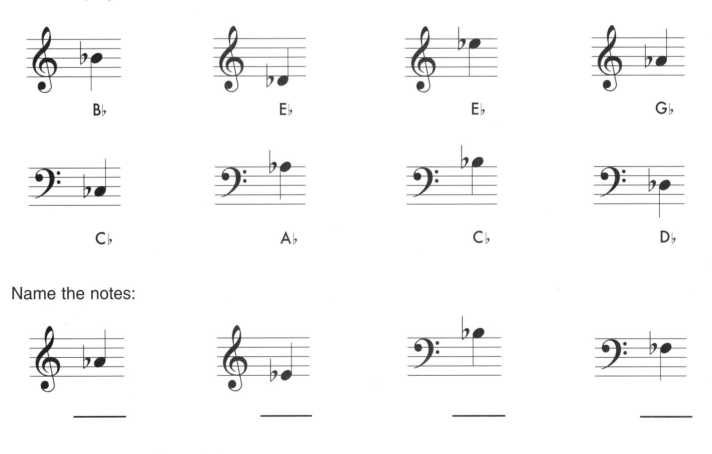

B♭   E♭   E♭   G♭

C♭   A♭   C♭   D♭

Name the notes:

____   ____   ____   ____

Which of these flatted notes is a **white** key? _____

Half Steps

Kangaroos and Half Steps

Kangaroos also like half steps (from 1 key to the very next key.)
Use this keyboard to help you with the following activity.

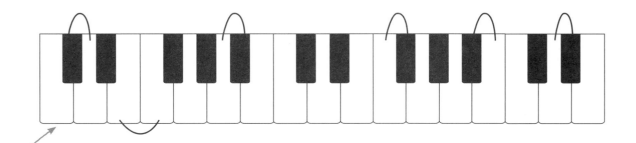

- Name the notes.
- Then draw an arrow from each pattern that matches above.

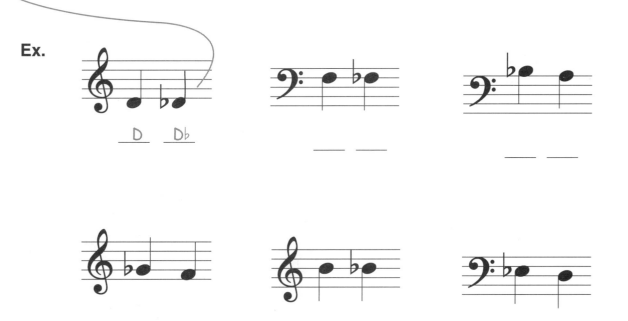

Juggling Flats

Place the correct number
next to each flat key.

Again, place the correct number
next to each flat key.

14

The Bunny and Kangaroo Hop

Help the bunny by connecting the lines to every **half** step.

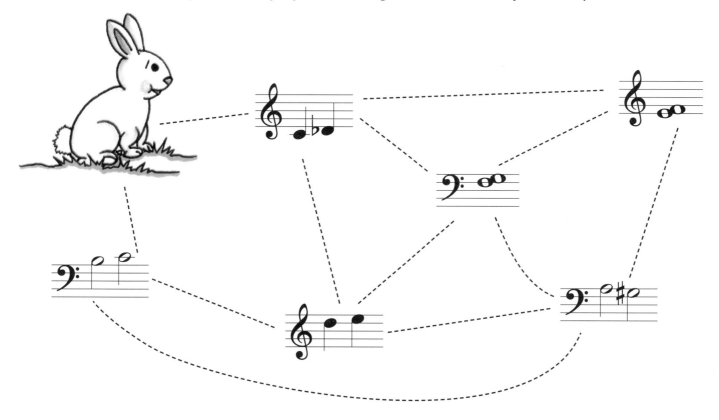

Help the kangaroo by connecting the lines to every **half** step.

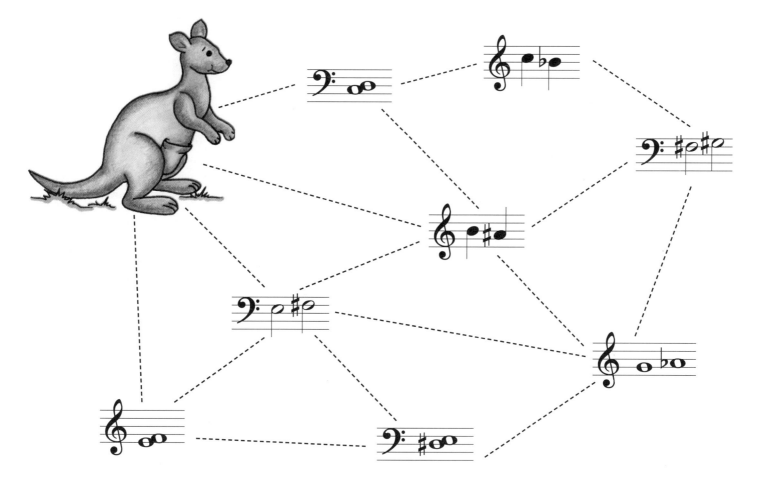

Hidden Picture No. 1

Color the following guide notes:

Treble: Middle C - **Yellow**; Treble G - **Orange**; Treble C - **Green**; High G - **Blue**;
Bass: Middle C - **Brown**; Bass F - **Red**; Bass C - **Blue**.

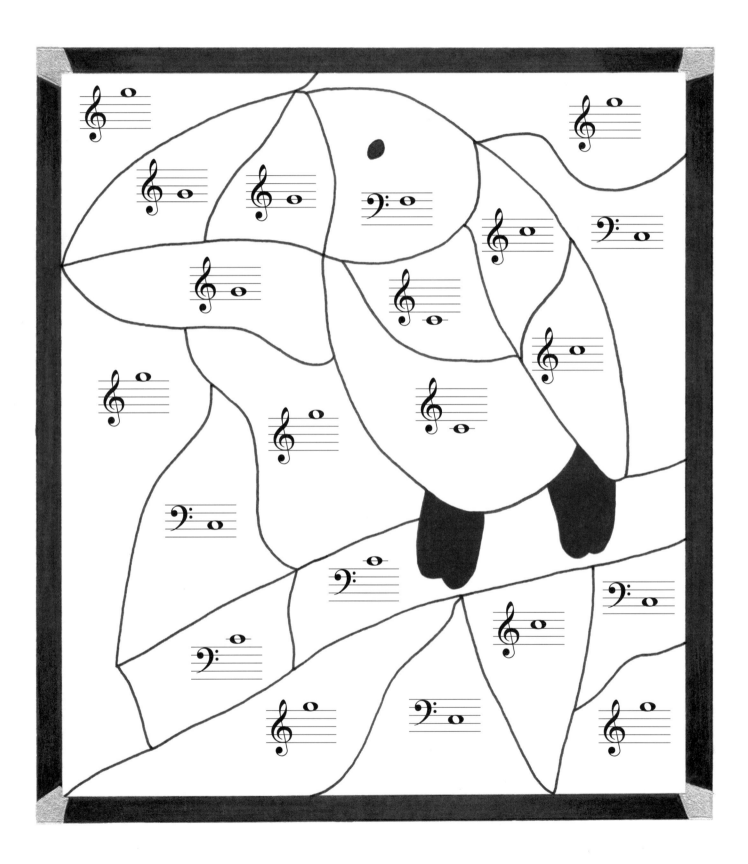

T-Shirt Patterns

- Write the missing note in the staves.
- Name the notes on the blank lines.
- Then play the notes.

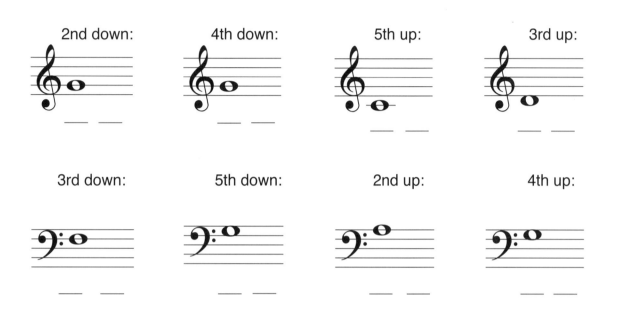

Name the patterns.

Ex.

5th down   _____   _____

Tonic and Dominant
I   V

Poolside Fun

Draw the notes:

Draw the dominant note from the tonic note on the Treble Staff.
The dominant is always a 5th up from tonic. Use quarter notes.

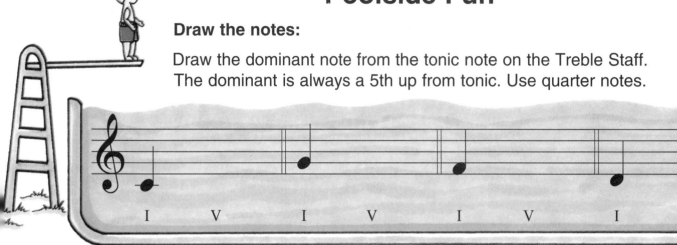

I   V   I   V   I   V   I   V

Below, circle the notes that show a I and V pattern.

FJH2329

Hidden Picture No. 2

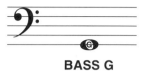

BASS G

Color all the areas containing Bass G **brown**.

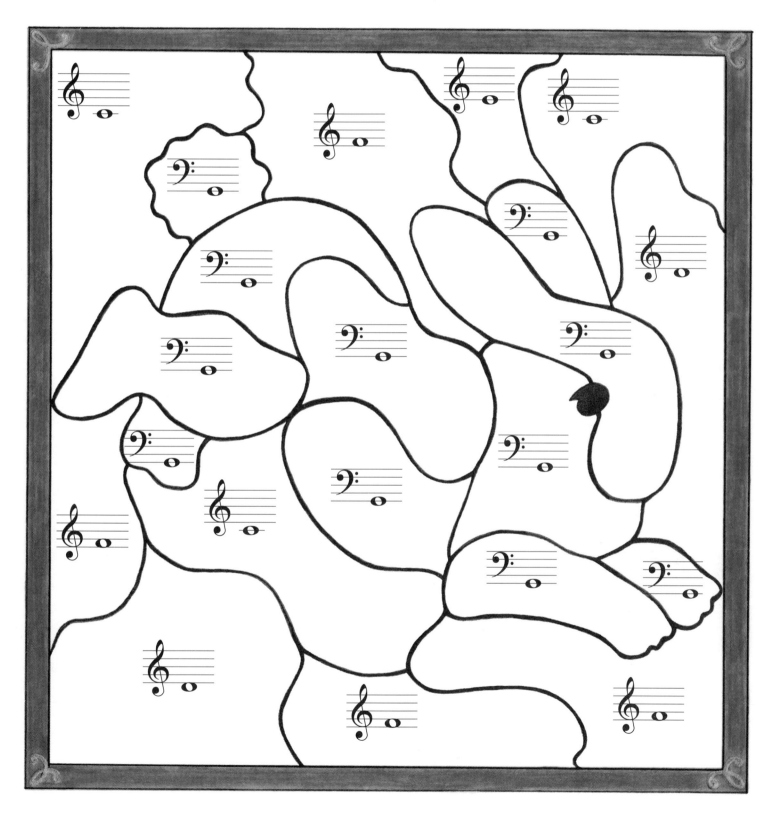

Bass G Position

On Board the Spaceships

Draw the notes in each spaceship. Then name each broken interval.
Below each spaceship, write if the interval pattern goes up or goes down.

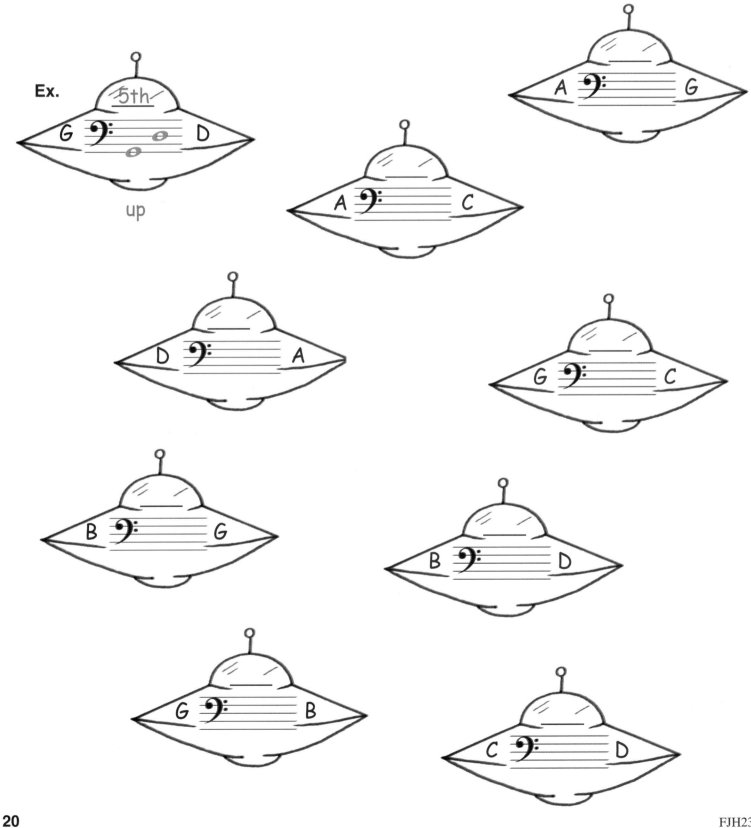

Prepare the parachutes to launch by drawing the intervals on each staff below.
Then, name each blocked interval.

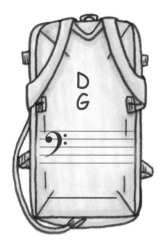
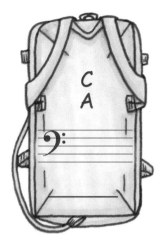
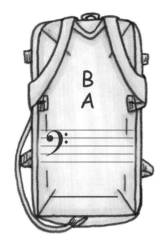
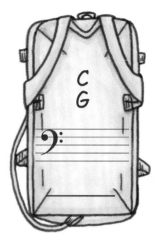

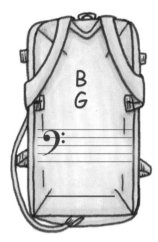
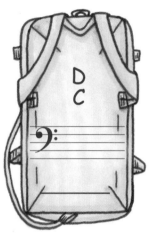
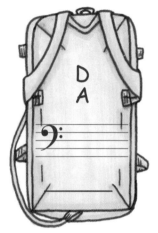
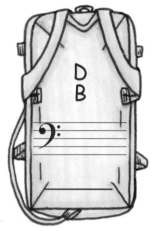

Circle the correct answer.

G♯   F♯

E♭   D♭

C♭   C♯

A♭   B♭

An Ice Cream Treat

How quickly can you name these notes in Bass G position? Time yourself.

Minutes? _____ Seconds? _____

Once you're finished, have an ice cream cone! ☺

FJH2329

Bass G Position

Cactuses and Tumbleweeds

Match each tumbleweed to the correct cactus. Then name the interval on each cactus.

Notes and Intervals
A Hole in One!

Name the notes in each golf ball. Then match the interval in each golf ball by writing the number in the correct green. An example has been done for you.

Ex.

#1

C   G

#2

#3

#4

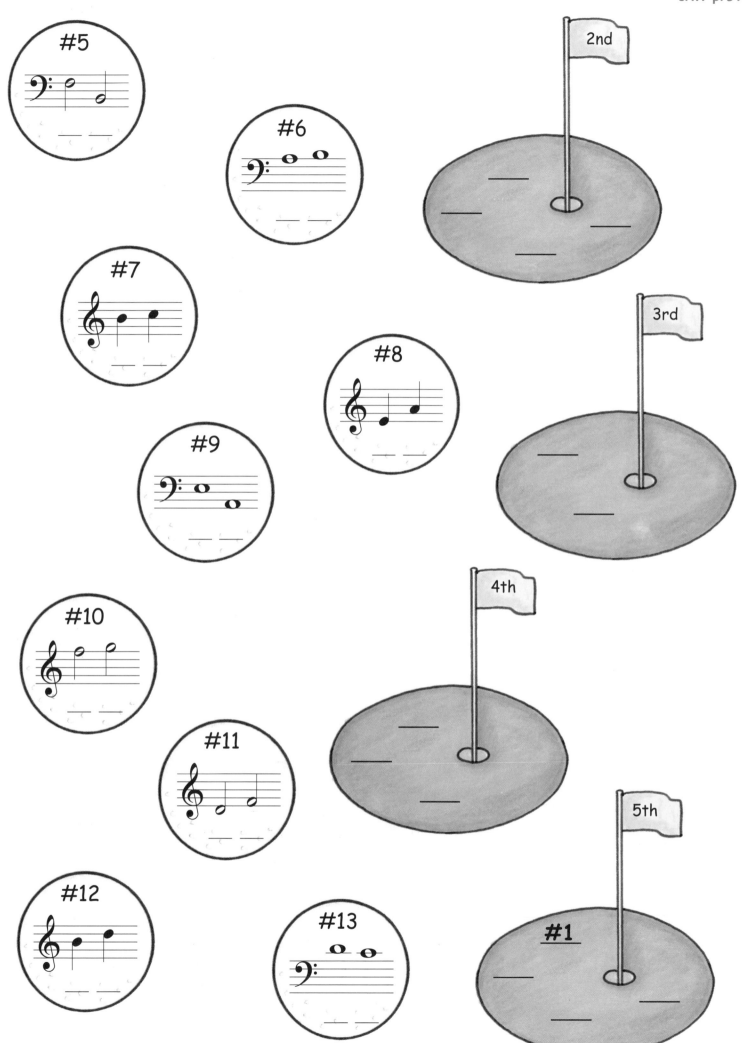

C Chord
Treasure Chest Hunt No. 1

"X" out the coins that do not contain the C I chord.

I chord

I chord

Tonic and Dominant in C

This is a **I** "one" chord in C: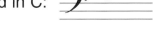

This is a **V⁷** "five-seven" chord in C:

- Draw a line from every **I** chord to the daisy.
- Draw a line from every **V⁷** chord to the tulip.

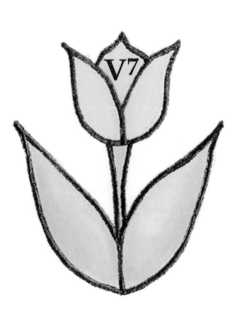

Now play the
I and **V⁷** chords
in C.

Note Review
A Detective Challenge

Now th_t I know st_ _ _ _to,   I_ _ _ to,

m_ _zzo   _ort_,   _n_   m_ _zzo

pi_ no,   l_ _ n   pl_ y

_ _ _thov_ n   _or   _ll to   h_ _ r!

G Chord

Treasure Chest Hunt No. 2

"X" out the coins that do not contain the G **I** chord.

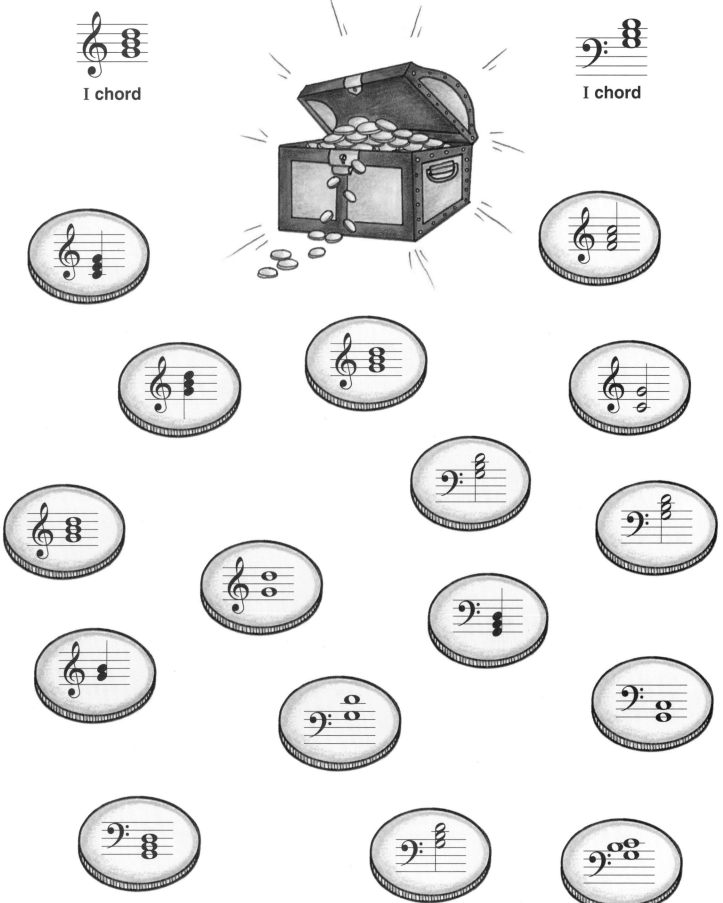

I chord

I chord

Grand Staff Notes

Name the notes. Then match the word in the right column to the word in the left column.

— — —

— — —

— — — —

— — — —

— — — —

— — — —

— — —

— — — —

— — — —

— — — —

— — —

— — — —

FJH2329

Sharps and Flats

It's Someone's Birthday

- Write the name of each note.
- Then play the notes.
- Lastly, draw a string from each balloon containing a ♯ or a ♭ to the matching child.

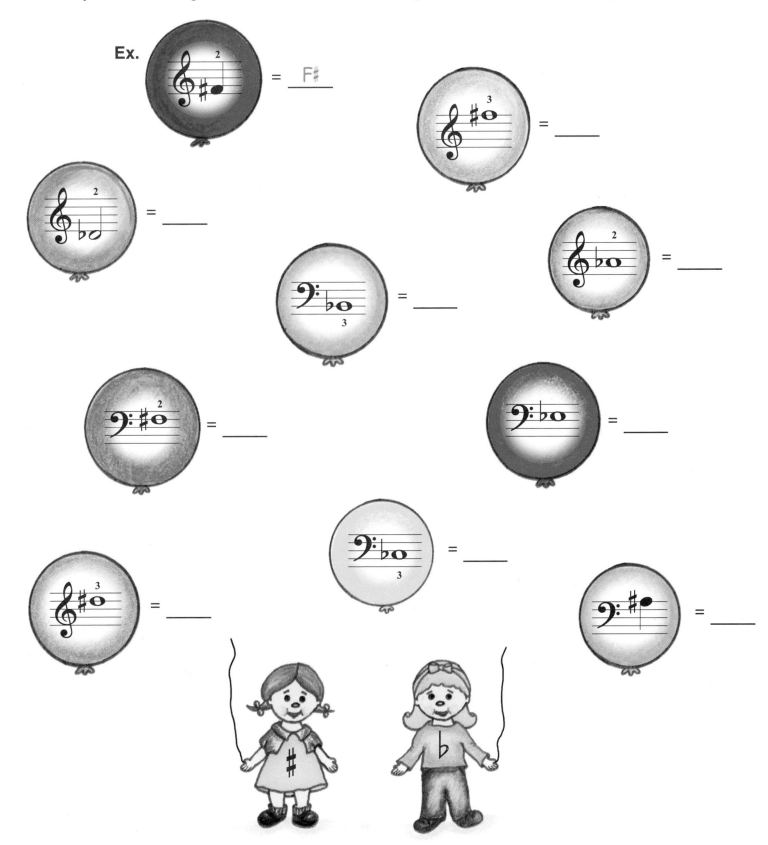

Certificate of Achievement

_____

Student

has completed

Succeeding with a Notespeller

GRADE 1B

You are now ready for

GRADE 2A

T H E
F·J·H
MUSIC
COMPANY
I N C.

Frank J. Hackinson

_____
Date

_____
Teacher's Signature